CAN

T.K.Virdee

Can You Outrun A Hippo??

Did you know one of the most deadliest places in the world is a place nick named "Snake Island".

What are elephants scared of?

What has to be broken before you can use it?

Did you know that elephants can't Jump?

What is Put on a table, but is never eaten?

What can you hold in your left hand but not in your right?

What has 8 eyes, 8 legs, and 8 hands?

Can you dig a tunnel through the earth to get to the other side?

ELBOW?

WARNING

AN ABSOLUTE MIND BLOWER

BE PREPARED

T.K.Virdee

CAN YOU LICK YOUR ELBOW?

A fantastic mind blower for the family, full of Gross, Weird and Interesting Facts, Riddles, Lateral Thinking Mind Boggling Puzzles, Tongue Twisters, Memory Games, a Myth Buster and much more.

Get ready to gross out all of your friends with these hysterically, nauseating, eye popping facts about all things gross, discusting, and gruesome.

CAN YOU LICK YOUR ELBOW?

Who ever said learning couldn't be fun. This is a terrific way to develop your childs mind without them even knowing their learning.

These Mind Bogglers will keep them and you, on your toes. A great way to bond with your friends and family. Youll be shocked to see who knows more. Don't say I didn't warn you.

Happy reading.

CAN YOU LICK YOUR ELBOW?

T.K.Virdee

CAN YOU LICK YOUR ELBOW?

CONTENTS

DID YOU KNOW............

Did you know a person produces about half a litre, to one and a half litres of farts a day? You're probably thinking, how many farts is that. Well, the average human being farts 14 times a day. What a stinker! Thankfully, we have air freshener.

How can the number 4 be half of five? This is a tricky one, think about it, but I bet you wont guess. The answer is this-

Start with FIVE, then take the F away. Then take the E away. That's half of FIVE gone.

Your left with IV. The roman number for four.

Told you you wouldn't guess it.

Did you know that your nose makes about 1 litre of snot everyday?

If you can smell something bad it because the stinky molecules have gone right into your nose. Ewww

 Did you know that jellybeans are so shiny because they are coated with shellac, which is made of insect poop? Yuck

Have you ever tried to fit the length of a can of coke in your mouth. Probably not because it seems pretty impossible. But Francisco Domingo Joaquim can. Yes, he does have a wide mouth, which measures 17 cm (6.69 in).   In 2010, The Guinness World Records named his mouth the largest one in the world.

Did you know that there are over 30,000 different varieties of fish in the world?

Did you know that snot is made up mostly of water?

Can you believe babies have more bones than adults. An adult has 206 bones, but a new-born baby has nearly 300 bones in her or his body. This is because babies have more flexible cartilage (in case your wondering what cartilage is, its a firm tissue softer than bone) in the body. As the child grows, some of the cartilage hardens and turns to bone, and some bones fuse together, which is why as adults we have less bones.

Did you know that the speed of a sneeze is approximately 100 mph? That's faster than a cheetah can run.

Did you know that the moon is moving away from the earth by 1.5 inches every year?

What has to be broken before you can use it?
-An egg!

What do you get if you cross a sheep with a kangaroo?
-A Woolly Jumper.

I found out today that I have an identical twin brother. I got very emotional.   When we finally met, I was beside myself.

 Do you hate the taste of your mouthwash?

Well, The Romans would use imported Portuguese urine; yes, that's right, imported wee, as mouthwash.

It was so popular that Emperor Nero had to tax it. It was a popular mouthwash until the 18th century. Yuck!

And if you hate the taste of mint toothpaste, you should know that the Romans used powdered mouse brains as toothpaste. Ewwww.

Now think how lucky you are.

What word would you use to describe a man that doesn't have all his fingers on one hand?

-Ordinary, most people have half their fingers on one hand!
What is always coming, but never arrives?
-Tomorrow!

Do you know that an octopus can lay 56,000 eggs at one time? They reproduce at 1 time and then die shortly after.

What can you catch but never throw?
-A cold!

 Did you know that a giraffe's tongue can be up to 21 inches long?

A hat, a scarf, a carrot, and 5 black pebbles are found on Jimmy's lawn. Nobody put them on the lawn, but there is a logical explanation to why they are there. What is the reason?
-There was once a snowman there.

The moon is not round like the earth but is similar to an egg shape.

Did you know the darker side of the moon is actually turquoise?

If there were no moon, our days would be 6-8 hours long.

 Did you know a teaspoon of honey is the life work of 12 bees?

The earth's circumference is 24,900 miles.

Did you know that tiger's legs are so powerful, that they can remain standing even when dead?

Horses live for around 25-30 years.

Did you know if your boogers are white, you're drinking too much milk? Yuck

Did you know Buckingham Palace has 775 rooms, and 78 bathrooms? Imagine having to clean all of them rooms, no thank you.

The White House in Washington DC has 132 rooms and 35 bathrooms. Nowhere near as big as Buckingham palace.

 Have you ever noticed that some

people are born with an extra hole in their ear? It's a little hole that sits right where the cartilage meets the face. This is a condition called preauricular sinus and scientists believe it may be an "evolutionary remnant of gills." How cool is that?

Did you know you fart enough in a day to fill a medium sized balloon?

Not as simple as you think.

Your doctor gives you 3 pills, and tells you to take one pill every half an hour. How much time would have passed by the time you take the three pills.

Have you guessed? Are you sure your answer is correct?
-The answer is actually 1 hour!
You start by taking 1 pill (the 1st pill). Half an hour later you take another (the second pill).
After a further half an hour (an hour in total), you take the last pill. (The third pill). So, it's actually 1 hour.

Did you know that humans could never land on Jupiter, Saturn, Uranus or Neptune because they are made of gas and have no solid surface?

A bee's sting is so strong that it can go through the thick hide of an elephant.

Did you know an octopus has three hearts?

Tigers live for around 15 years in the wild, but when in captivity can live for 20-26 years.

Did you know snails are born physically attached to their shells?

Did you know that elephants can't Jump?

The worlds heaviest elephant weighed 11,000KG.

What are elephants scared of? Anything moving around their feet, as well as bees.

A lion can live for 10-14 years in the wild but when in captivity it can live for as long as 30 years.

Do you know that only 1% of your fart smells? 99 % of the gases in your fart do not smell?

Did you know the Aldabra giant tortoise can live between 80-120 years?

Did you know Wilbur and Orville made the first aeroplane in the world in 1903. They did four small flights?

What animal has 32 brains?
-Leeches have an amazing 32 brains.

Vultures are pretty gross. Did you know that when vultures are hot, they cool themselves down by excreting on their own legs? Yes, that's right, pooing on there own legs. They also live on rotten flesh, and they prefer it that way. Yuck.

Flies are also pretty gross. They eat faeces, yes that's poo. Then loads of bacteria is transported on to their bodies, including typhoid. And, the next bits worse. They then land on your food.

They also lay there eggs on dead flesh which turn into maggots. Gross!!!

Did you know that the earthworm has 5 hearts?

 Did you know that the light bulb was invented in 1879? That's the same year Albert Einstein was born.

Did you know that first steam powered rail journey took place in 1804?

Did you know the worlds largest chocolate bar was made in 2011 and weighed 5,7925 kg? Yummy all that chocolate.

Where do fish keep their money? -Riverbanks!

What is it easy to get into, but hard to get out of? -Trouble!

Mr Brown was killed on Sunday afternoon. Can you help solve the mystery?

The wife said she was reading a book. The butler said he was taking a shower. The chef said he was making breakfast. The maid said she was folding clothes, and the gardener said he was watering the plants.

Who killed Mr Brown?
-The Chef!
Mr Brown was killed in the afternoon, but the chef was making breakfast.

 People buy me to eat, but never eat me. What am I?
-Cutlery!

A garden snail has about 14,000 teeth, and other species of snails can have over 20,000 teeth.

Farts travel at about 9.5 km/hr.

The gas that make your farts smell is called hydrogen sulphide.

Do you know it is possible to light a fart on fire? Think about it, it's a gas. I wouldn't advice you to try it.

You don't want to set you bottom on fire.

Did you know even once dead you can still let off burps and farts for up to three hours?

In some cultures, burping after a meal is considered as a compliment to the chef.

Have you ever wondered how long you can burp? The longest burp ever recorded was 1 minute, 13 seconds, and 57 milliseconds in 2009.

The loudest burp ever recorded was 109.9 decibels in 2009.

Did you know most people burp between 6-20 times a day?

Dave had a job and was paid £10.00 an hour.

He really hated the job so found another job, but that job paid him 50% less so he decided to take a pay cut.

He liked the new job, but then got bored so found another job, which paid 50% more than what he was currently earning.

How much was he being paid at the third job?

-If you said £10.00

You're wrong. Sorry.

The answer is actually £7.50. I know it's a little confusing.

His first job paid £10.00

His second job 50% less- £5.00

His third job paid 50% more than his 2nd job, which paid £5.00-which is £7.50.

Did you know cow's stomachs have four compartments? Often referred to as 4 stomachs.

Did you know that the burps of 10 cows could heat a small house for a year? That is a lot of heat. Think about global warming.

Now this one you can most definitely try. Did you know you could catch a fart in a jar, and let it out later? Eeww.

 Did you know sharks grow up to 50,000 teeth in a lifetime?

Baby sharks are born with all their teeth.

Do you know that bananas float in water?

Did you know that trees are the longest living life form on earth, and never die from old age?

Do you know that as well as having unique fingerprints, we also have unique tongues?

There are more stars in space than there are grains of sand on a beach.

 The oldest animal in the worlds is Jonathan; he is 183 years old and is an Aldabra giant tortoise, living in St Helena, near West Africa.

The oldest tree in the world is over 4,700 years old, and is nick named Methuselah. It is a bristlecone pine tree in California.

Did you know slugs have four noses? Like me, you must be thinking why does it need 4 noses?

 Did you know that a hippopotamus can run faster than a human?

The tallest tree in the world is 115.54 metres that's 379.1 ft. Its called the Hyperion and is in the Redwood national park, in California.

The longest human fingernail in the world is 909.6 cm. That's almost 10 metres long. Now that must have been hard to manage.

Did you know that worms don't have eyes?

The widest tree in the world is 38 feet in diameter. That's wider than the length of two giraffes.

 Did you know pigs can't look up into the sky?

Did you know that the queen has two birthdays? That means double presents of course.

Have you ever found that the sound of someone laughing often makes you laugh? Laughter is contagious, and the sounds of laughter often trigger laughter. A good laugh has great short term effects. It can energise many organs, boost your intake of oxygen rich air, stimulate your heart, your muscles, and lungs, and increase the endorphins that are released by your brain. Even a fake laugh can lift you mood, so feel free to laugh your head off. Ha ha ha pop.

What month of the year has 28 days?
-All of them!

Did you know that kangaroos cant walk backwards.

Did you know that the first comic superhero was The Phantom?

Superman was the first comic book super hero to appear in his own television series.

What is full of holes, but still holds water?
-A sponge!

Did you know that tardigrades are the toughest animals on earth and they can go without food for 30 years.

What is a tardigrade? This is a tardigrade-

They are also known as water bears, or moss piglets.

They live for up to 2.5 years. They can survive extreme low and high temperatures, radiation, and even chemicals. They have even been into space, and it is believed that they are the only animals that can survive in space.

On the 11th April 2019, The Beresheet lunar spacecraft crashed. At the time there were thousands of microscopic, dehydrated tardigrades aboard. Wonder if there still up their.

The first Disney movie was Snow White and the Seven Dwarfs, released in 1938. That's the same year Terry Wogan was born. Prince Charles was born 10 years later in 1948. That's how old Disney is.

The largest tree the world is called The General Sherman Tree and it is 84 metres tall, and 36 feet in diameter at the base, and its still growing.

Did you know that tomatoes and avocadoes are actually fruits, not vegetables?

What goes up and down but doesn't move?
-A staircase!

What has a head, a tail, but no body?
-A coin!

Where does one wall meet the other wall?
-On the corner!

Did you know that about 70% of the adult body is water?

Did you know that your nose and your ears continue growing throughout your entire life?

Now are you left handed, or right handed, or are you ambidextrous? If you are right-handed, count yourself lucky, right-handed people live, on average, nine years longer than left-handed people do.

Sorry to disappoint you left handers, and as for you ambidextrous people, well you will just have to wait and see.

Did you know that the number 4 is the only number that has the same amount of letters in its word form?

Did you know that a tiger's skin is also striped, like its fur?

If you got me, you want to share me; if you share me you haven't kept me, what am I?
-A secret!

If you are running in a race, and pass the person in second place, what place are you in?
-Second place!

Did you know that horses and cows actually sleep standing up?

Did you know that Coca-Cola even sells soup?

I belong to you but other people use me more than you, what am I?
-Your name!

I am always hungry, and will die if not fed, whatever I touch will soon turn red, what am I?
-Fire!

Mr and Mrs Barnaby have 6 daughters, and each daughter has one brother. How may members of the Barnaby family are there?
-If you said 14 don't feel bad, it's the wrong answer.

The actual answer is 9. The daughters share 1 brother (the same brother).

So, there's 6 daughters, 1 son, and Mr and Mrs Barnaby.

Did you know that the largest cave In the world is Han Son Doong, in Vietnam? Its over 200 metres high, and has its own climate, rivers, and jungles Inside.

Did you know that lightning can strike twice?

Did you know that 1 quarter of your bones are in your feet?

A man dies of old age on his 25th birthday, how is this possible?
-He was born on 29th February!

Did you know that your blood is as salty as the ocean? About 85% of the sodium in your body is found in blood and lymphatic fluid. Sodium helps regulate the fluid balance in your body and assists in the function of nerves and muscles.

 Did you know that a hagfish could throw up 17 pints of mucus on a predator? Yes, throw up as in vomit. Now that is discussing, I wouldn't want to annoy a hag fish, and would advice you to stay well away too. But if you have any enemies, a hagfish may make the perfect birthday present.

A man is looking at a photo of someone. His friend asks who it is. The man replies, "Brothers and sisters, I have none. But that mans

father is my father's son". Who was in the photo?
-His son!

Do you like raisins? Did you know that raisins contain 40 mg of sand and grit in every 100 grams?

What words are pronounced differently by just capitalising the first letter?
-Many words are, but this is just a couple- polish and Polish, scone and Scone. Can you think of any more?

I have no voice, yet I speak to you. I tell you all things in the world that people do. I have leaves, but I am not a tree, I have pages, but I am not a bride. I have a spine, but I am not human. I have hinges, but I am not a door. I have told you all, I cannot tell you more. What am I?
-I am a book!

Did you know that oregano legally contains 1,250 insect parts in 10 grams? Yuck.

A lift is on the ground floor. There are 4 people in the lift including me. When the lift gets to the 1st floor, one person gets out, and 3 people

get in. Then the lift goes to the second floor, and 2 people get out, and 6 people get in. Then it goes to the 3rd floor, no one gets out, but 12 people get in. The lift then  goes up again, and half way the cord snaps, and the lift crashes. Everyone in the lift dies. How did I survive?
-I got out on the second floor!

Did you know that tortoise blood was once used to get rid of tooth ach and clean your teeth and mouth?

Did you know that your kitchen sink contains more bacteria than a toilet?

Just think how many germs your mum and dads kitchen sponge has on it.

Do you wear headphones? Well, wearing headphones for an hour can increase the bacteria in your ears by 700 times.

Do you sleep with your mouth open? Did you know that in the course of an average lifetime, whilst sleeping you might eat 70 assorted insects, and 10 spiders or even more?

 Do you know that one in every six mobile Phones have faecal matter on it? Mobile phones carry 10 times more bacteria on them than a toilet. Just think how much you hold it, and even put it on your face. If you are still addicted to that mobile, at least sanitise it. Yuck.

Did you know that cat's urine glows under a black light? Yes, that's right, cats pee.

Did you know that the average yawn lasts six seconds?

You saw me where I never was and where I could not be, and yet within that very place, my face you often see. What am I?
-A reflection.

What question can you never answer yes to?
-Are you asleep.

You walk into a room that contains a match, a kerosene lamp, a candle, and a fireplace. What would you light first?
-The match.

Did you know that the average male lion weighs 180 kg, the average female lion weighs 130 kg, and the heaviest lion on record was 375 kg? That's heavier than a large vending machine.

A lion can run up to speeds of 50 mph. That's just a little slower than a truck drives on a motorway.

 Did you know that boiled toads were once thought to cure rheumatism?

Ewww.

Do you know anyone that wets his or her bed? Over 400 years ago, rotted mice were fed to children to cure bedwetting. That's disgusting, but its one way to stop your younger brother and sister wetting their bed. Yuck!

A bus driver was heading down a street; he got to the end of the street, and passed a stop sign without stopping. He then turns the wrong way on a one-way street, and comes to another road. There is a "No left turn" sign, which he completely ignores and turns left anyway. He passes 2 police cars, and isn't stopped once, because he didn't break any traffic laws. How can this be?
-He was walking.

Did you know that more than 1,000 thunderstorms take place on earth every minute? Now if I said every hour that would be far more easier to believe, but it is actually over 1,000 per minute, now that is a shocker. And if that's not amazing enough, read on.

How hot is a lightning bolt?
-Very hot, lightning can heat the air it passes through to 50,000 degrees Fahrenheit (5 times hotter than the surface of the sun). Woww

I am an insect, the first half of my name is another insect. What am I?
-A Beetle (bee tle).

How large is the sun in comparison to the earth? Well, one million earths can fit inside the sun.

I build up castles, I tear down mountains, and I make some people blind. What am I?
-Sand!

If you drop me, I'm sure to crack, if you smile I'm sure to smile back. What am I?
-A mirror!

What building has the most stories?
-A library.

Did you know that it's impossible to hum when holding your nose? Try it.

Bats are the only mammals that can fly.

Wombats are the only animals that have cube shaped poop. This is because of how their intestine is shaped and forms poop. So, if you see cube shaped poop you know a wombat has been around.

Did you know that the roar of a lion can be heard from 8 km away? That's about 5 miles, so if you hear the roar of a lion, be aware, there somewhere near, and can run pretty fast.

You probably don't want to test this one out, but your stomach acid is seriously strong. I mean seriously strong.

Your blood has a pH level of around 7.4., which is slightly alkaline. On the other hand, your stomach acid is around a pH level of 1 -3, which is highly acidic. You're protected from it thanks to your stomach's protective lining. In fact, the acid in your stomach can even dissolve razor blades. Now a fact like that is a shocker.

Have you ever wondered why Granma and grandpa smell funny?

Sorry grandparents, no offense.

Well, firstly don't worry, you're not imagining it. And secondly, yes, your right, it wouldn't be polite to ask them why they smell. So here it is.   The reason is this.   Your body odour can change throughout your life, and usually does.

Think about a new-born baby. They have that distinct, fresh scent. Now, think of a teenage boy. They, too, have a distinct scent that's very different from a baby. Sorry teenage boys but you too have a, let's just say "different smell".

Older adults like our mums and dads, aunties and uncles are no different. Many describe their scent as being mildly sweet and musty.

And now for the grandparents. They also have a unique smell. Just to confirm, age related changes in body odour are likely to have nothing to do with personal hygiene. Instead, experts think it is the result of odour compounds and bacteria interacting on the skin.

The major odour compound responsible is called 2-nonenal. While environmental and lifestyle factors can also influence body odour, 2-noneal appears to be responsible for the distinct, slightly musty odour which sticks to older people, or should we say the Grandparents. Either way, it has nothing to do with personal hygiene, so need to be to worried.

Do you know what a hybrid animal is? It's an animal that is born from two different species. On the earth, we have many hybrid animals.

Do you know what a "Tiglon or Tigon" is?   It's a hybrid offspring of a male tiger and a female lion.

The offspring of a male leopard and a female lion is called a "Leopon".

There is also the "Jaglion", which is the offspring between a male jaguar, and a female lion.

A "wholphin" is extremely rare. It's the offspring of a female bottlenose dolphin, and a male false killer whale.

A Zorse is the offspring of a zebra stallion, and a horse mare.

A zonkey is a cross between a zebra and a donkey. Donkeys are closely related to zebras and both animals belong to the horse family. Zonkeys are very rare.

A "Pumapard" is the offspring of a puma and leopard. In the 1980's and 1900's two hybrids were born in Chicago.

The offspring of a male lion and female tiger is called a" liger".

A "Grolar bear" is the offspring of a grizzly bear and a polar bear.

 A "Cama is the offspring of a male camel and a female llama.

A "Savana cat" is a hybrid of a domestic feline and a medium-size African wild cat.

For those of you that love roller coasters, you are not the only ones. But have you ever stopped to think about what is happening to your insides? If not, I can tell you some scriously weird stuff Is going on inside your body when you're being flipped around.

Amusement park rides literally shake and toss your internal organs around. Yes, that's why you get the horrible sickening feeling in your stomach, which is also caused by a change in force, experienced by your organs. People tend to feel dizzy or nauseated on rides because our brains receive conflicting messages from the motion-sensing organs in our bodies, including our inner ears and eyes.

Do you know what the worlds largest toy store is called, and where it is located?

Hamleys is the oldest and largest toy store in the world, and its located here in the UK. Yes, that's right, in London. It was named after William Hamley the founder in 1760. That's more than 260 years ago.

How big is it? Well, in London UK it has seven floors covering 54,000 square feet. And if that is not eye-popping enough, you'll be pleased to know that a giant Hamleys has opened in Beijing. Its 115,000 square feet and covers 5 floors.

Have you ever seen a new born baby cry? You may have notice that there crying involves a lot of red-faced wailing and nothing else. No tears at all. And no, its not because they're just pretending, so they'll get attention.

Its actually because their tear ducts aren't fully developed yet. They do gain the ability to cry properly should we say, eventually, but for the first several weeks of a new-born's life, they produce just enough tears to keep the eyes moist, but not enough to form tears that run down their adorable little cheeks.

Why did the nurse need a red pen at work?
-In case, she needed to draw blood.

Have you ever wondered what species are king of the earth? Well, I'm not sure about king, but around 80 percent of known species on the earth are actually insects. Beetles form the largest insect group with around 360,000 known species and many, more that haven't been discovered/ named.

Did you know that the Sahara dessert is the third largest dessert in the world, and is the largest hot dessert in the world?

How big is the Sahara dessert? Well, it's almost the same size as china, and takes up 8% of the earths land. It is an amazing 9.2 million km2.

The hottest temperature ever recorded in the Sahara was 136 degrees Fahrenheit (57.77 Celsius) in 1922. That's really hot.

What has many keys but can't open a single lock?
-A piano!

Have you ever heard of the word cyborg.? Do you know what a cyborg is?

A cyborg is someone whose physical abilities are extended beyond normal human limitations by mechanical elements built into the body. Doesn't that sound cool?

Neil Harbisson, is a cyborg artist. He is best known for being the first person in the world to have an antenna implanted in his skull, and for being legally recognized as a cyborg by a government.

Neil was born with the inability to see colour. The Cyborg Antenna is a sensory system, which allows him to feel and hear colours as audible vibrations inside his head, including colours invisible to the human eye like infrareds and ultraviolet. And if that doesn't sound amazing enough just read on.

He later had an updated model of the eyeborg implanted. His new model not only can sense 360 different colours and pick up ultraviolet and infrared frequencies; it also has WiFi and Bluetooth connectivity.

Now how brilliant is that? So just imagine, his friends can use an app to send images directly to his gear so he can "see" them without using his eyes. Wowww, now that is cool.

You may be wondering if cyborg animals exist, and the answer is yes.

These are sometimes called bio-robots or robo-animals.

They can be considered as cyborgs as they are combination of an electronic device with an organic life form.   Several species of animals have been successfully controlled remotely. These include moths, beetles, cockroaches, rats, dogfish, sharks, mice, and pigeons, and even cyborg plants exist.

Did you know that hippopotamus milk is pink? Can you imagine, pink milk, how cool is that? Wouldn't like to drink it though. Yuck!

What can you hold in your left hand but not in your right?
-Your right elbow!

I am the beginning of the end, and the end of time and space. I am essential to creation and surround every place. What am I?
-The letter "E".

What are the minimum amount of cuts you need to cut a pie into eight pieces?
-you can do this in three cuts.

1st cut) 1 Centre cut (you have 2 pieces)

2nd cut) Stack the halves on top of each other and cut again. (you now have 4 pieces)

3rd cut) stack the 4 pieces of pie on top of each other, and do you final cut. (you now have 8 very messy pieces of pie)

A small welsh town has the longest town name in Europe. The town is called-

"Llanfairpwllgwyngyllgogerychwyrndrobwllllantysiliogogogoch".

Yes, it really is called that, what a mouthful.

Well done if you manage to say it. It has 58 letters. You can call it Llanfairpwll for short.

Do you chew your fingernails? How about your toenails? Did you know that 10% of kids admit to chewing

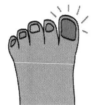 their toenails? Yuck. They must be pretty flexible.

Did you know that Queen Isabella of Spain in the 15th century bragged that she had only bathed twice in her life? Phewww I wouldn't want to stand near her.

Did you know that part of Einstein's brain is on display in a museum in Philadelphia? Eww.

The more you take, the more you leave behind, what am I?
-Footsteps!

What room do ghosts avoid?
-The living room?

Three doctors said that Robert is their brother. Robert says he has no brothers. Who is lying?
-No ones lying. Robert has three sisters, who all happen to be doctors.

Add 1,000 to 40. Add 1000 again, then add 30. Add 1000 again, and then add 20. Add another 1,000, and then add 10. What did you get?

2 + 1 = 3

If you said 5,000 you are wrong.
The answer is 4,100.

How did I work it out? Well,

1000+40=1040

1040+1000+30=2070

2070+1000+20=3090

3090+1000=4090

4090+10=4100.

I speak without a mouth and hear
without ears. I have no body, but I
come alive with the wind. What am
I?
-An echo!

Did you know that the word " SWIMS
" still spells swims up side down?

Did you know that the longest TV
advert in history was 14 hours long?
It was aired in Brazil and you can
watch it online if you really bored.

 Did you know that China cloned an
award winning police dog?

Did you know what people in Britain use to use to wake up, before alarm clocks were accessible?

There were people called "Knocker Uppers". That is actually, what they were called. During the industrial revolution, their job was to go around waking people up by knocking on their doors with a wooden stick.

I do wonder though, who woke them up. Just imagine if they woke up late.

Did you know that a Wimbledon tennis ball is always stored at room temperature? Yes, that's right, they are stored at 68 degrees Fahrenheit, as the temperature of a tennis ball affects how it bounces.

On average, we breathe 20,000-22,000 times a day.

 Did you know that sea otters hold hands when they sleep to prevent them from drifting apart? Aww

You are escaping a labyrinth, and there are three doors in front of you. The left door leads to a pit of crocodiles. The middle door leads to a a pool of lava. The right door leads to a lion that's not eaten in five months.

What door do you take?

-The door leading to the lion that's not eaten in five months. The lion would be dead.

Do you know who discovered penicillin?
-It was Alexander Fleming.

 If I am holding a bee, what do I have in my eye?

I have beauty in my eyes. Beauty lies in the eye of the beholder. (bee holder).

If you turn me on my side I am everything, but if you cut me In half im nothing. What am I?
-The number 8!
(on the sides looks like infinity, but in half looks like 0.)

Did you know who the first female doctor was?

The first female Doctor was born in Bristol, England in 1821. She became a doctor in America 1849 and her name was Elizabeth Blackwell.

Is coral a plant or an animal?
Take a guess.
If you said a plant your wrong, sorry.
If you said animal, your right.

Corals are animals, not plants. They use their tentacles to catch tiny animals called zooplankton. They sting their prey using special cells they have called nematocysts. That's why if you go diving your told to stay away from the coral, because it stings and cause abrasions and, in some cases, can be poisonous (zoanthid and zoanthus corals). But coral as well, are very fragile animals, and if you accidentally kick, stand on or touch them you can damage or even kill them.

Coral grows by building coral reefs, and the biggest coral reef in the world is The Great Barrier Reef off Australia. It is around 1400 miles long. That's around the same length as 750 male giraffes standing on top of one another.

Just in case your wondering, Male giraffes are around 18ft tall, and female giraffes are around 14ft tall.

Giraffes also have 3 hearts.

Do you know the first female Prime Minister in England was Margaret Hilda Thatcher (1979)? She was also known as "The Iron lady", and "Margaret Thatcher the milk snatcher".

Mrs Roberts went to the police and claimed that her Diamond necklace was missing. When the police arrived, they saw no signs of a break-in. Only one window was broken, everything had been turned upside down, and was a mess and, there were dirty footprints all over the floor.

The next day the Police arrested the culprit for fraud.

Who was it?

- Mrs Roberts! The glass had been broken from the inside. If it had been broken from the outside, there would have been glass on the floor inside!

Now for the big question you have all been waiting for. Can you lick your elbow?

Do you know that most people think it is impossible to lick your own elbow? Try it!

In fact, most people can lick their own elbow, the inner part of the elbow. But, if I asked you can you lick the outer part of your elbow, the bony part, the answer for most people would probably be, no.

You may be surprised but licking the outer part of your elbow, the bony bit, is not impossible. People who have short upper arms, or long tongues, or who are very flexible can lick the outer part of their elbow. Its pretty impressive. So why not put it to the test and challenge your friends and family to see who can lick their outer elbow. Can you?

Did you know that a vampire bat slurps half of its body weight in blood each night? They drink their victims' blood for about 30 minutes. Scary.

Darren is placed in a cold damp cell, with a muddy floor, and only one window positioned so high, that no one can reach it.

 The cell is pretty much empty. There is only a shovel, a small paper basket, and a blanket. He has no food or water and will not get any. He has 2 days to escape. Digging a tunnel is not an option, because it will take over 2 Days.

How will he escape?

-Darren should shovel a pile of mud under the window, climb onto it and escape from his cell!

Did you know that Florence NIghtingale was considered the founder of modern nursing? She introduced good patient care and hygiene. She was born in Italy in

1820 and died at the age of 90 in 1910.

Do you know that the first female Prime Minister in the world was elected in 1960? She was the Prime Minister of Sri Lanka, and then The Dominion of Ceylon.   Her name was Sirimavo Bandaranaike.

Do you know that nearly 2,400 types of bacteria have been found living in people belly button? Yuck!

There are two types of belly buttons. There are innie's and outie's. Innie's are more common.

Most people have belly buttons, but rarely it is actually possible to be born without one.

Did you know that half of all bank robberies take place on a Friday?

Do you know that grapes explode when you put them in the microwave? They can even light on fire. Please don't try this without an adult.

Did you know that hippos lips are 2 feet wide? They have massive smiles.

Do you know how to make your home-grown tomatoes sweeter?

-Sprinkle a little baking soda on to the soil around them. Once grown your tomatoes will taste extra yummy.

Do you know it's impossible to sneeze without shutting your eyes?

Do you know how to peel a boiled egg perfectly? It's easy. Just add 1 teaspoon of baking soda into the water before boiling. The shell will come off effortlessly.

A woman called Tina is in a room. Her challenge is to open a bottle of wine without breaking it. The only thing in the room is a knife, a hammer, a spade, a tea towel, a screw and a table. She cannot ask for any help or leave the room.

What should she do?

-Use the hammer to insert the screw into the cork of the bottle. Then use the other side of the hammer to remove the screw, by pulling it out. There you go, she's opened the bottled.

Do you know how to make your phone sound louder?
-Put it inside a tall empty glass.   It works a treat if you need to crank up the volume on your alarm! How does it work? Easy. The sound waves bounce around a little
and are directed up and out, amplifying the volume a little more, making it sound louder.
Did you know that Mc Donald's once invented bubble gum flavour broccoli? Well, that's one way of getting the kids to eat their green.

Do you know you can separate the yolks in your eggs, just using an empty water bottle? It's pretty cool. Try it.

Break an egg into a bowl. Then take an empty water bottle. Remove the lid and slightly squeeze it and dip it into the bowl of egg. Release the squeeze, and your yolk should be in the bottle. Just like magic. Who would have thought it could be so easy.

 A boy is told that he will receive £10.00 if he manages to water some flowers in his neighbour's garden, without flooding her flowers. The problem is she has just a super powerful hose, that blasts water really fast, and has no sprinkler. There is no watering can either. What should he do?

-Take an empty milk bottle and insert small holes into the lid, by heating the tip of a nail and piercing the lid several times. Then fill the bottle up with water and screw the lid on. There you have it, your home-made watering can!

What do you if you get chewing gum on your clothes?

-You can freeze the clothing, and when the chewing gum is frozen, peel it off!

-Or you can place some cardboard over the chewing gum, and iron the back of the garment. It should transfer on to the cardboard.

And when it gets stuck in your hair, cut it all off, or yell for help.

Only kidding.

You can use smooth peanut butter.

First tie up the rest of your hair, so it's out of the way.

Rub a spoon of peanut butter on to the chewing gum, massage and work through with a comb.

The peanuts break down the gum, and the butter works as a lubricant to help extract it.

Now if you manage to get super glue in your eyes, then you will have to yell for help.

Did you know that there are more life forms living on your skin, than there are people living on this planet? That's right, germs, mites and bacteria. Yuck!

Do you anyone with stinky sweaty feet? Do you know your feet can actually sweat over a pint per day?

Did you know that when you die, the bacteria in your gut that helps you digest food will eventually start to digest you?

Humans shed around 50- 100 hairs per day.

Do you know why the atmosphere is so dusty?
-Dead skin accounts for a billion tons of dust in the atmosphere.

The human skin sheds around 30,000-40,000 dead skin cells every minute. Humans lose 200,000,000 skin cells every hour. During a 24-hour period, a person loses almost five thousand million skin cells. That's almost 9 pounds (4 kilograms) of cells every year!

Why cant a women living in Europe be buried in Canada?
-Because she is living! She can't be burled anywhere.

Complete these series of numbers-If

9=4, 10=3, 21=9, 24=10, 8=5, 7=5, 99=10, 100=10, What does

16=?   17=?

-The number is equal to the number of letters in their spelling. .i.e. 16 =7 (sixteen)

Mrs Barnetts bungalow was decorated completely pink. The carpet was pink, the curtains were pink, the furniture was all pink. What colour were the stairs?
-There were no stairs. It was a bungalow!

Did you know that black apples are actually real? They are actually black, and white on the inside like any other apple.

There are also pink bananas that are edible. They are called Musa Velutina.

 A woman dressed in all black is walking down a country lane, and suddenly a large black car with no lights comes around the corner, and screeches to a halt. How

did the car driver know she was there?
-It was daytime!

You are driving a bus. The bus is empty when you begin. At the first bus stop, 4 people get on. At the second stop, 2 get off and 5 people get on. At the third stop 1 person gets off and 6 people get on. What colour are the bus drivers' eyes?
-What colour are your eyes? You are driving the bus.

Did you know that Einstein's brain was stolen when he died?

Do you know that there was a prehistoric dragon fly, that's wings stretched around 2.5 feet? Around 300 million years ago the Meganeura lived on the earth, and is known to be the largest flying insect to exist on the earth.

Did you know that it is actually illegal to own just one Guinea pig in Switzerland? This is because guinea pigs are social animals that prefer companionship of other guinea pigs.

Is it legal for a man to marry his widow's wife?
-I don't know, but seeing as he's dead it would be hard for him to do so!

What goes up but never comes down?
-Age!

A woman has two sons, they were born on the same hour, the same day, on the same month, on the same year, at the same place. However, they are not twins, how is this possible?
-They were triplets, they also had a sister.

After a crocodile has enjoyed a good meal, it can go without food for 3 years. It preserves its energy by staying motionless.

Scorpions can go 1 year without food. They eat one-third of their body weight in just one meal.

A Galapagos tortoise can also survive one year without food. They have a slow metabolism and have large internal storage for water.

A ball python go up to 6 months without food.

Bears can go for more than 3 months without, eating, drinking, exercising, or going for a number 1 or 2 (the wee or poo). Yes, that's right. This is why they are known as great hibernators.

Elephants can go for 4 days without water and can smell water from a 5-kilometre distance.

Did you know that the dodo bird was a flightless bird with a hooked beak? In colour, they were brown, grey, black, and white. Dodos were recorded as being naturally curious, friendly birds.

They lived on the island of Mauritius, and it is believed that Dutch settlers first saw them in 1598. Until humans discovered the island, the dodo had no natural predators. 65 years later, they became extinct.

It's commonly believed that the dodo went extinct because Dutch sailors ate them all, after finding that they were incredibly easy to catch due to the fact it had no fear of humans. It is believed that the last dodo bird was seen in 1662.

Did you know that it is believed that the tallest dinosaur was the Brachiosaurus group of sauropods.

The brainiest dinosaur was the Trodden. It was a hunting dinosaur.

The heaviest dinosaur was the Argentinosaurus at 77 tons. That's the equivalent of 17 African elephants. It was also the longest dinosaur, and it is believed to be the largest land animal to have ever lived.

Did you know that an elephant trunk has around 40,000 muscles?

A human has less than 850.

Did you know that dolphin mamas sing their own name to their calve before they are born?

Bananas glow blue under black lights. Cool.

Only a quarter of the Sahara Desert is sandy.

Did you know that the woolly mammoths were still alive when the Egyptians were building the great pyramids?

Did you know that the slimy coating on snails and slugs protects them from friction?

They can actually crawl over the sharp edge of a razor blade without being harmed, due to their thin layer of mucus. Now that is impressive!

Did you know that the common swift bird can fly for 10 months without touching the ground?

Here's some fun experiments for you to try at home.

If you want shiny looking 1 pence and 2 pence pieces, soak them in some tomatoes ketchup overnight, and see how amazing they look in the morning.

What causes them to shine like brand new? well- As your coppers are exposed to the environment, your pennies become coated with a layer of copper oxide, making them look tarnished (with a dull, brown, dirty appearance). The acid in the vinegar from the ketchup reacts with the salt to remove copper oxide, which is what was making your pennies dull. .

Did you know that water could travel? Try this experiment.

Take 5 cups and fill them up ¾ with water.

Then take some food colouring and add a different colour to 3 of the cups.

Now arrange them in a line with the clear water between each coloured cup.

Take 4 sheet of kitchen towel and fold them to make them long.

Dip each end of the kitchen towel into a cup, forming bridges and wait to see water travel.

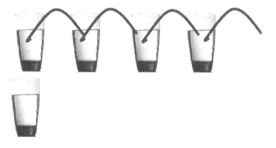

Did you know that oil and water do not mix, oils are hydrophobic, that means that they are "water fearing"?

You can make your own lava lamp using just this.

Vinegar or ketchup

Take an empty clear water bottle and fill it with 2/3 of vegetable oil.

Fill the rest of the bottle with water, leaving just a little space at the top.

The oil will then float to the top as it is heavier and has a higher density.

Don't mix.

Now add some food colouring. This colour will only mix with the water not the oil.

Then get your grown up to give you a Alka-seltzer tablet and break it into four pieces.

Take each piece and add it into the bottle and watch what happens. You can put the lid back on to the bottle and try it a few days later if you like. All you need is some more Alka-seltzer tablets.

Eating too many carrots can make your skin orange or yellow. This is called carotenemia.

Did you know that no number from 1 to 999 contain the letter "A" in word form. That is actually quite impressive considering the letter "A" is used in so many words.

The tongue is covered with 8000 taste buds.

You blink about 20 times per minute.

You measure 1 cm taller in the morning than you do before you go to bed. This is because the cartilage between your bones get compressed and squashed throughout the day, making you slightly shorter.

Billys mum has five children. The first is called Lillo, the second is called Laura, the third is Lina, the fourth is called Lili. What is the fifth child's name?
-Billy!

It's as light as a feather, but the strongest person can't hold it for more than 5 minutes. What is it?
-Breath!

I am big on Saturday and Sunday.
I am small on Tuesday, Wednesday, and Thursday. I am not on Monday and Friday.
What am I?
-The letter "S"!

I am white when I am dirty, and black when I am clean. What am I?
 -Blackboard!

What do the letter T and
an island have in common?
-Both of them are in the middle
of waTer.

Which creature walks on four legs at first, two legs after, and three legs later?
Man – four limbs as a toddler, two feet as a youngster, two feet and a walking stick as an elderly man.

One night, a man received a call from the Police. The Police told the man that his wife was murdered, and that he should get to the crime scene as soon as possible. The man immediately hung up the phone and drove for 20 minutes. As soon as he got to the crime scene, the Police arrested him for murder.

How did the Police know that the man committed the crime?
-The police did not tell the man where the crime scene was!

What starts with the letter T, is filled with T and ends in T?
-A teapot

The person who makes it, sells it.
The person who buys it, does not use it. The person who uses it, doesn't know he is using it. What is it?
-A coffin!

Two mothers and two daughters went out to eat. Everyone ate one burger, yet only three burgers were eaten in all. How is this possible?

-They were a grandmother, mother, and daughter!

Do you know how long it would take a snail to crawl 1 mile? It would take about 220 hours.

Did you know that whales actually have belly buttons? How cool is that, can you imagine how big it would be?

What invention lets you look right through a wall?
-A window!

The worlds lightest mammal is a bumblebee bat, which weighs about as much as 2 m&ms.

Say Racecar backwards.
- "Racecar"!

A cockroach can live for over a week without a head.

My Name is Fudge. I live on a farm. There are 4 other dogs on the farm with me. Their names are Snowy,

Pinky, scruffy, and Brownie. What do you think the fifth dogs name is?
-Fudge!

Name four days in the week that start with the letter "T".
-Tuesday, Thursday, Today, and Tomorrow.!

If u multiply or divide me by any number, the answer you get will always remain the same. What number am I?
-I am Zero!

Do you know that ear wax was once used as lip balm?

I am a three-digit number. My second digit is four times bigger than my third digit. My first digit is three less than my second digit.

0 1 2 4 5 6 7 8 9 10

What number am I?
-141!

If four people can repair four bicycles in four hours, how

many bicycles can eight people repair in eight hours?

-16 bicycles!

What word has five letters but sounds like it only has one?   - Queue!

What starts with a "P" and ends with an "E" and has thousands of letters? - Post office!

Imagine you are in a room filled with water. There are no windows or doors. How do you get out?
-You stop imagining!

Bill phones his manager in New York. Phone calls to New York are charged at the rate of £2.90 for a 5-minute call.

How much would an 11-minute call to New York cost?
-An 11 minute call costs £6.38!

5 people can paint a fence in 3 hours. How long will it take 6 people to

paint the same fence (Assume everyone works at the same rate).
- It would take 6 people 2 hrs 30 minutes!

12 men take 5 days to build a road 100m long. How many days will 20 men take to build a similar road which is 400m long?
-12 days.

I can fall off a building and live, but in water I will die. What am I?
-Paper!

What is far behind us, and can be seen without looking at it?
-The past!

I am the reason you run. I am the reason you scream. I am the cause of your pain. I am a cage from which you will never be free. What am I?
-Your body!

Does anyone you know want to be a doctor? Well, many years ago, doctors would have had to taste their patient's urine and snot in order to diagnose them. And if you think that's bad enough, read on.

For thousands of years, medical practitioners believed that sickness was the result of a little "bad blood".

Medieval doctors prescribed blood draining as a treatment for just about everything, whether it was a sore throat or even the plague. Some barbers offered blood drainage along with haircuts and shaves. And if that's not bad enough, sometimes leeches were even used to suck the blood directly from the skin.

What was this insane remedy called? It was called bloodletting. Medical physicians like Hippocrates and Galen believed the human body was filled with yellow bile, black bile, phlegm

and blood, which needed to be kept in balance.

Now for the most gruesome part.

More than 7,000 years ago, a surgery called trepanation was used to treat epilepsy, headaches, abscesses, blood clots, and release evil spirits believed to possess the sick and mentally ill.

What is trepanation? It's when holes are drilled or scraped into the skull. Yes, that's right, and some patients actually  survived. Believe it or not, in some cases it is still used today, but is called craniotomy and is not used for the same reasons.

And now things go from gruesome to gross. Most disgusting of all, the ancient Egyptian physicians used human and animal excrement (urine and poo) as a cure and remedy for diseases and injuries.

Lizard blood, dead mice, mud and mouldy bread were all used as ointments and dressings. Papyrus, donkey, dog, and gazelle poo were considered to have healing properties and the ability to ward off bad spirits.

Have you ever heard of corpse medicine? Yes, it's as disgusting as it sounds. It actually contained human flesh, blood or bones, and was used for hundreds of years.

The Romans believed that the blood of dead gladiators could cure epilepsy.
These cannibalistic medicines were thought to have magical properties. The belief was that by consuming the remains of a deceased person, the patient would digest part of their spirit, leading to increased energy and wellbeing.

Skull was used for migraines, and human fat for muscle pain, and mummy powder was used to cure bruising. Now that's crazy medicine.

A boy and his father get into a car accident. When they arrive at the hospital, the doctor sees the boy and exclaims "that's my son!" How can this be?
-The doctor is the boy's mother.

If a brother, his sister, and their dog weren't under an umbrella, why didn't they get wet?
-It wasn't raining!

What travels around the world but stays in one spot?-A stamp!

Where can you find cities, towns, shops, and streets but no people?
-A map.

This is a tricky one.
If you manage to get it well done.

"A word I know, six letters it contains, remove one letter and 12 remains, what is it?"
-Dozens!

How many letters are there in the English alphabet? Take a guess and I bet the answer you have, is different to mine. Did you say 26? Well, actually there is 18.

How did I work that out?
(3 letters in "The") (7 letters in "English") and (8 letters in "Alphabet".)

Mr. Blue lives in the Blue house.
Mrs. Yellow lives in the Yellow House.
Mr. Orange lives in the orange house.
Who lives in the White House?
-The President!

Are bogeys safe to eat?
Look, if your nose is going to all that effort of creating a snack, the least we can do is check out its nutritional value.
(Yes, they're safe. Chew away!)

These words all describe the word "big". Can you guess them?

1. As***n*m***l
2. *n*r***s
3. Gi**n**c
4. M*s***e

Answers
    1. Astronomical, 2. Enormous
    2. Gigantic 4. Massive.

Have you ever wondered what comes after 1000 , no I didn't mean 1001. lol

Name of no.	Amount of 0 after 1 short scale.	How you write it
One hundred	2	100
One thousand	3	1000
Ten thousand	4	10,000
100 thousand	5	100,000
1 million	6	1000,000
1 billion	9	1000,000,000
1 trillion	12	
1 quadrillion	15	
1 quintillion	18	
1 sextillion	21	
1 septillion	24	
1 octillion	27	
Googol	100	
Googolplex	10^{100}	
Grahams no	G64	Too big to explain
Tree (3)		A number so large its beyond our ability to express.

What about infinity?

Infinity is not actually a number. It basically means endlessness, where as a number defines an amount.

Have a look at this cool number pattern.

$$1 \times 8 + 1 = 9$$
$$12 \times 8 + 2 = 98$$
$$123 \times 8 + 3 = 987$$
$$1234 \times 8 + 4 = 9876$$
$$12345 \times 8 + 5 = 98765$$
$$123456 \times 8 + 6 = 987654$$
$$1234567 \times 8 + 7 = 9876543$$
$$12345678 \times 8 + 8 = 98765432$$
$$123456789 \times 8 + 9 = 987654321$$

What type of bow can never be tied?

-Rainbow

Do you know what a blizzard is?

Well, it is a really heavy snowstorm. Officially, to be classed as a blizzard it would have winds of 35 mph or more, last more than 3 hours.

Now, if you were to ever be in a situation where you get caught in a blizzard be prepared. You could lose electricity, hot water and heat.

Here is some free advice, blankets, flashlights, extra batteries, and candles are handy to have lying around the house and walking anywhere or driving in a car should be avoided.

Have you ever heard the word Tsunami? A Tsunami is a natural disaster. It is when a wave from the ocean travels inland. The waves build up higher and higher on the land, and the ocean level decreases.

What causes a tsunami?

Well, it is caused by sudden motion on the ocean floor. Like a disturbance in the sea surface. For example, due to an earthquake near the ocean floor or below the ocean, or large volcanic eruption near the ocean. They can take place due to a fast moving under water landslide, or landslides entering the water, or even a meteorite.

The force creates waves that move in an outwards direction, creating long waves in the ocean that go over land.

They usually occur in the Pacific Ocean and recently the Mediterranean Sea.

Have you ever wondered what an avalanche is?

Avalanches are huge amounts of snow, ice, and rocks that fall rapidly down the side of a mountain. They can be deadly.

What causes the snow to fall? Well, it can be due to many things. For example, rain, earthquakes, rock fall and icefall under the snow due to it weakening over time.
Have you ever heard of a volcano? A volcano takes place when there is an opening in the earth's crust.

Through the opening Lava, volcanic ash, and gases escape. Lava is like super-duper hot semi fluid rock.

It looks a little bit like a mountain that opens at the top.

Eruptions can be explosive or effusive.

Have you ever heard of a tornado? Tornadoes are one of the most violent and powerful types of weather.   A tornado is also known as a twister. Tornadoes are made up of a very fast rotating column of air that usually creates a funnel shape. The funnel-shaped cloud extends from a thunderstorm to the ground with whirling winds that can reach 300 MPH.

 Tornadoes can occur when a warm front meets a cold front, forming a thunderstorm, which then can create 1 or more "twisters."

Do tornadoes take place on land or sea? Well, have you ever heard of a waterspout?

Tornadoes and waterspouts have a lot of similarities, they are both a tower of powerfully rotating wind. The main difference is that waterspouts happen over water and tornadoes tend to happen over dry land.

Once a tornado hits the ground, it may continue for a few seconds or as long as three hours.

A tornado moves about 30 miles an hour and usually, travels less than six miles before dying out.

If you are unfortunate enough to be faced with a tornado on your doorstep, here is some free advice. If you are indoors, take cover in the cellar or a small space, or even in a bathtub because it is heavy and typically well-secured. Stay in a windowless room on the lowest level. Hopefully, you won't ever be faced with a situation like that.

And if you're wondering what the difference is between a tornado, and a hurricane, read on.

The biggest differences between hurricanes and tornadoes are how big they are and how long they last. Tornadoes and hurricanes are similar in that they both contain strong rotating winds that can cause damage.

Hurricanes develop over warm seas and are usually 150 KM or over wide.

Hurricanes can not form over l and.

They need warm, humid air, found only over the ocean in tropical areas, for it to form. A typical hurricane lasts anywhere from 12 to 24 hours, but can last for as long as a month, as Hurricane John did in 1994.

What happens when a hurricane hits land? Well, they strengthen over water and weaken over land. This is because its deprived of the warm water it needs to power itself.

Do you know that the Box jellyfish has enough venom to kill 60 adults? Even though the Jellyfish doesn't have the most potent venom in the world, it can kill you in 15 minutes.

Mosquitoes are so deadly, they are estimated to kill about 725,000 people every year. Malaria alone affects around 200 million people a year, and around 600,000 people a year die. You must be thinking, why are we now talking about malaria. What is malaria? Malaria is caused by the Plasmodium parasite. The parasite can be spread to humans through the bites of infected mosquitoes. Who would have thought that a mosquito could be so dangerous?

What has lots of eyes but cannot see?
-A potato!

What has many teeth but cannot bite?
-A comb!

What is cut on a table but is never eaten?
-A deck of cards!

What has one eye but can't see?
-A needle!

What has many needles but does not sew?
-A Christmas tree!

Riddle: What has hands but cannot clap?
-A clock!

What has legs but does not walk?
-A table!

I have no life, but I can die, what am I?
-Im a battery!

A panda walks into a restaurant. He sits at a table and looks at the menu and orders his food. When he finishes it The waiter comes over, the bear takes out a gun shoots the waiter, then leaves. Everyone is in shock. A policeman then runs after him and asks him why he shot the waiter.

The bear says" look me up in the dictionary".

The police man slightly confused looks up panda in the dictionary, it says-
"Panda: Eats, shoots and leaves".

Did you know one of the most deadliest places in the world is a place nick named "Snake Island".

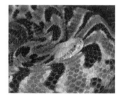 It is called IIha Da Queimada Grande, and is an island 25 miles off the Brazilian coast. The island is full of venomous golden lancehead pit vipers . There are over 4,000 vipers on the island alone, it is so deadly that even local wont dare to go there, and the Brazilian government has made it illegal to visit there. The Golden pit viper is one of the most deadliest snakes in the world.

Another deadly place you would definitely not want to visit, is Turkmenistan Darvaza. It is known as the "Gates of Hell." It is a natural gas field that was set on fire to prevent methane gas from spreading, and it has been burning since 1971.

Yes, that's right. The gas is still burning, as natural gas cannot be trapped. They expected the process to take a few weeks, but the flames have been burning ever since. In fact, scientists still do not understand how much natural gas there is.

Where is this place? It is in the middle of the Karakum Desert, about 260 kilometres north of Turkmenistan's capital.

It has boiling mud, and orange flames in the large crater, 70 meters (230 ft) in diameter. Now That is deadly.

Can you believe that even a lake can be deadly?

The Lake Natron acts a lot like a lake of fire. The lake's high levels of Natron, sodium carbonate make its waters damaging to human skin and eyes as It can reach ph. level of over 12. The water's alkaline comes from the lake's sodium carbonate.

Temperatures at the lake, mostly reach above 40 °C (104 °F) but can reach 60°C. Lake Natron can kill a human, but flamingos breed on its salty water.

The circumference (the distance all the way around the equator) of the earth is 24,901 miles.

The earths diameter (the distance from one side of the earth to the other through the centre is 7,926 miles.

How long would it take you to travel from one side of the earth to the other?

If you dug a tunnel all the way to the other side of the earth and wanted to travel through it, it would take about 42 minutes and 12 seconds to reach the other side.

When falling down towards the centre of the earth, you would be accelerating constantly, due to gravity.

By the time you reach the halfway point, after falling for 21 minutes, you would be traveling at 28,000 kilometres per hour.

Once you crossed the halfway point, the velocity would carry you back up the other side of the tunnel for another 21 minutes. This time, however, gravity is slowing you down, so by the time you reach the other end, you come to a perfect stop, just as you arrive at your destination.

Can you dig a tunnel through the earth to get to the other side?

Well. I won't leave you in suspense.

No, it's not possible. Sorry to disappoint you all. This is because; you would have to dig through:

More than 8,000 miles of solid rock and molten magma.

You would face temperatures up to 6,000 degrees.

Extreme pressures up to 300 million times more than what we experience on earth's surface.

So no, digging a tunnel straight through the earth is not actually possible.

How long would it take to walk around the world?

The earth is 24,901 miles. If you walk an average of 3 mph, it would take you 8300 hours if you didn't stop and you kept up that pace.

That is 345 days. That of course is impossible as you would have to stop to go for a number 1 and 2 and eat, drink and of course shower, sleep and rest.

Did you know that pirates really did exist and still do today?

Blackbeard was really a pirate and was the most feared out of them all.

TONGUE TWISTERS.

Now lets see how good you are at tongue twisters.

Try these few with you friends a family, and see who can say it the fastest, the most times.

Here goes-

"I scream, you scream, we all scream for ice cream."

"I saw Susie sitting in a shoeshine shop."

"If a dog chews shoes, whose shoes does he choose?"

"Can you can a can as a canner can can a can?"

"I have got a date at a quarter to eight; I'll see you at the gate, so don't be late."

Now let's try something harder.

"Peter Piper picked a peck of pickled peppers. A peck of pickled peppers Peter Piper picked. If Peter Piper

picked a peck of pickled peppers,
where's the peck of pickled peppers
Peter Piper picked? "

"Betty Botter bought some butter
But she said the butter's bitter
If I put it in my batter, it will make
my batter bitter
But a bit of better butter will make
my batter better So it was better
Betty Botter bought a bit of better
butter. "

Now were they hard?

Here's a few more.

"How much wood would a woodchuck
chuck if a woodchuck could chuck
wood? He would chuck, he would, as
much as he could, and chuck as
much wood, as a woodchuck would if
a woodchuck could chuck wood."

"Fuzzy Wuzzy was a bear,
Fuzzy Wuzzy had no hair,
Fuzzy Wuzzy wasn't very fuzzy, was
he?"

"She sells seashells by the seashore.
And the shells she sells by the
seashore are seashells for sure."

"Red lorry, Yellow lorry

Red lorry, yellow lorry"
Say this as fast and as many times
as possible.

"Betty's big bunny bobbled by the
blueberry bush."

Say this as fast and as many times
as possible.

"Six sticky skeletons."
Say this as fast and as many times
as possible.

"Green glass globes glow greenly."
Say this as fast and as many times
as possible.

"A really leery Larry rolls readily to
the road."

"Rory's lawn rake rarely rakes really
right."

"Lucky rabbits like to cause a
ruckus."

"I looked right at Larry's rally and left
in a hurry."

"Round and round the rugged rocks
the ragged rascal ran."

"If you must cross a course cross cow across a crowded cow crossing, cross the cross coarse cow across the crowded cow crossing carefully."
"Brisk brave brigadiers brandished broad bright blades, blunderbusses, and bludgeons — balancing them badly."

"Six sick hicks nick six slick bricks with picks and sticks."
"The thirty-three thieves thought that they thrilled the throne throughout Thursday."

"I thought a thought.
But the thought I thought
Wasn't the thought I thought I thought.
If the thought I thought I thought,
Had been the thought I thought,
I wouldn't have thought I thought."

Now for a real challenge. Get your head around this.-

"If one doctor doctors another doctor,
Then which doctor is doctoring the doctored doctor?

Does the doctor who doctors the doctor, doctor the doctor the way the doctor he is doctoring doctors?
Or does he doctor the doctor the way the doctor who doctors doctors?"
What a mouthful.

Tongue twisters are established to clarify the pronunciation of words and stretch and strengthen the muscles that we tend to use to talk.

They assist us to spot words and sounds we have trouble pronouncing. The more we practice, the better we get, so why not make it as fun as possible.

Why not see if you can create your own tongue twisters and test them out on your friends.

MEMORY GAMES

Have a look at these numbers, for 60 seconds.

5 9 8 7 2 5 3 6 4 1

Now cover them.

Do you think you can remember?

5 8 7 2 5 3 6 4 1

What number is missing? Try to remember.

Where was the number that was missing?

This was the number sequence.
5 9 8 7 2 5 3 6 4 1

Now try one slightly easier. Look at the numbers below for 30 seconds.

4 5 9 8 6 5

Cover the numbers up and try to say the numbers in sequence.

Well Done!

Want another challenge?
Look at these numbers for 60 seconds, then cover them up. Try to remember the following numbers in the correct sequence-

6 4 3 2 9 7 6 1 5 0

Could you remember them. If you could well done.
The average person can remember 7 numbers, and you've managed to remember 10.

Now try to remember the sequence and the list of these items. See how many you and your friends and family can remember.

Memorise these for 30 seconds, then cover them and try to remember the order, and items.

I went to the shop and brought some butter, eggs, sugar, self-raising flour, and milk.
Did you do it?

Now try this one. Memorise for 30 seconds then cover them.

I went to the shop and brought some paint brushes, paint, pencil, pens, and paper.

That was an easy one.

This is a slightly harder one.
Memorise the items for 90 seconds before you start the challenge.
I went to the shop and brought some bread, eggs, tea, coffee, milk, brown sugar, chocolate, tomatoes, cheese, coleslaw cucumber and ham.

Did you remember that?
Now try this challenge, its harder, but it is in alphabetical order.
Memorise these items for 2 minutes.

I went to the shop and brought -

An apple, a bat, a chameleon, a dragon fly, an Easter egg, a firefly, a grizzly bear, Hoola hopes, an ink pot, jelly babies, a koala bear, a Lamborghini, a Mars bar, nectarines, oranges, peaches, quality streets, a rabbit, a snail, tomatoes, an umbrella, vaseline, warm gloves, a xylophone, a yellow hat, and a zebra.

Well done. That was a hard one.

Ready for the next challenge?

Now look at the following stars and dashes for 60 seconds and try to remember the order. When your 60 seconds is up, cover the sequence and try to say what the sequence was.

✱✱✱＿＿＿✱✱＿＿✱＿✱＿✱＿

Did you manage to remember the sequence? Now try this one.

✱✱＿＿✱✱＿＿✱＿✱＿＿＿✱✱＿

Could you do it? It's not as easy as it looks.

Now try this one.

＿＿＿✱✱✱＿＿✱✱＿＿✱✱＿＿＿

Now let's see if you better at
memorising pictures.

Did you know that it is believed that
people can memorise pictures easier
than words as our brains can process
images 60,000 times faster than
words, and our brains process
pictures twice, and words once?

Look at this picture for 60 seconds
then cover it and answer the
questions.

Cover the picture up.
How many balloons were there?
Do you know?

Now try the same with the picture
below. Look at it for 60 seconds then
cover it?

Was there a star fish on the beach?
How many star fishes were there?
Was the man holding the beach ball
with one hand or two hands?

Now do this one. 60 seconds ok.

Answer these questions about the
picture.

How many people were walking
across the bridge?
How many trees were there?

Were there steps in the picture?

Now check. Did you get it right?
Well done!
Look for 30 seconds

Now cover it up.

How many circles was each tyre on the car made of?

Which window was bigger?

What way was the car going?

Now check. Did you get the questions right? Yes, there was a trick question, the windows were the same size.

Take 2 or 3 minutes to revise this.

Batman, Superman, Wonder Woman, the Incredible Hulk, Captain America, Iron Man,

Spiderman and Flash. (8 hereos)

Now you must try to remember and figure out what is missing from here. Cover the names of the superheroes up.

What is missing?

Batman, Superman, Wonder Woman, Captain America, Iron Man, and Flash.

Now do it again.
Elephant, lion, tiger, gorilla, monkey, giraffe, sea lions, penguins, and otters. (9 animals)

Cover them up.
What's missing?

Elephant, lion, tiger, gorilla, monkey, penguins, and otters.

Now check to see if you got it right.

The way you see things also has a part in how well you remember them.

Now look at this list and see if you can remember more when you see things displayed in a list, or clearer pattern.

Red
Purple
Pink
Blue
Green
Yellow
Brown
Black
Grey (9 colours)

Now cover them up.
Whats missing?

Red
Purple
Pink
Blue

Brown
Black
Grey

How about this one.

Guitar
Keyboard
Piano
Saxophone
Microphone
Drums
Tambourine
Xylophone
Triangle

Now cover them up.
What's missing?

Guitar
Keyboard
Saxophone

Microphone
Xylophone
Triangle

Elbow
Hand
Eye
Nose
Ear
Finger
Toes
Belly button
Teeth
Tongue

What 4 body parts are missing.

Elbow
Hand
Eye
Nose
Teeth
Tongue

Studies have shown that word
search and other puzzles can
help improve memory, focus,
vocabulary, and overall mental
sharpness. Let's see how good you
are at finding words.

WORDSEARCH

FUN

The Mind blower

C	S	P	U	M	A	P	A	R	D	Q	E	L	M
O	R	C	D	O	N	A	C	L	O	V	T	I	D
R	S	E	M	A	G	Y	R	O	M	E	M	C	B
P	B	N	C	R	T	I	G	L	O	N	E	K	L
S	D	U	R	I	D	D	L	E	S	F	S	Y	O
E	B	G	R	U	E	S	O	M	E	A	E	O	O
M	O	I	M	P	E	L	I	G	E	R	O	U	D
E	G	L	E	O	P	O	N	I	A	T	T	R	L
D	G	I	U	I	M	A	N	U	S	T	I	E	E
I	I	E	N	A	C	I	R	R	U	H	U	L	T
C	E	W	H	O	L	P	H	I	N	I	Q	B	T
I	E	C	Y	B	O	R	G	L	T	G	S	O	I
N	E	O	G	R	O	S	S	N	L	O	O	W	N
E	E	C	I	M	D	E	T	T	O	R	M	G	G

THE MIND BLOWER

MOSQUITO
RIDDLES
PUMAPARD
LICK YOU ELBOW
GRUESOME
VOLCANO
BOGGIE
CORPSE MEDICINE
BLOOD LETTING
ROTTED MICE
FART
WHOLPHIN
MEMORY GAMES
TIGLON
CYBORG
GROSS
TSUNAMI
LEOPON
HURRICANE
LIGER
BURP

TRICKY SPELLINGS

N	D	I	M	W	E	I	R	D	S	A	I	O	L
O	A	C	L	E	L	B	A	T	P	E	C	C	A
I	I	T	R	O	C	C	U	R	R	E	N	C	E
T	L	Y	T	C	A	D	O	R	E	T	P	H	Y
A	H	C	D	R	C	O	B	C	M	S	T	L	H
I	I	O	A	E	E	Y	E	N	P	N	E	U	A
C	A	P	A	O	F	S	I	L	E	R	A	Y	R
N	M	H	R	R	N	I	A	R	E	L	M	O	E
U	H	O	R	R	A	L	N	C	B	C	H	F	C
N	N	A	U	D	H	H	N	I	T	A	T	E	I
O	I	N	C	A	A	I	P	R	T	E	S	O	E
R	O	M	I	S	S	P	E	L	L	E	A	N	V
P	E	R	V	U	E	O	N	A	M	T	L	R	E
E	E	A	R	T	H	R	I	T	I	S	I	Y	T

TRICKY SPELLINGS

SINCERELY
PRONUNCIATION
WEIRD
MANOEUVRE
OCCURRENCE
DEFINITELY
PTERODACTYL
PHARAOH
ACCEPTABLE
ARTHRITIS
ASTHMA
MISSPELL
RECEIVE

CAN YOU LICK YOUR ELBOW?

O	S	U	U	V	M	S	F	E	N	U	R	O	S
M	R	N	E	H	L	U	N	W	R	S	M	E	M
I	O	N	O	E	N	N	H	T	R	A	E	E	I
N	B	R	R	T	S	N	E	E	Z	E	E	T	N
D	S	N	I	A	R	B	E	S	U	O	M	P	D
B	Y	W	J	E	L	L	Y	B	E	A	N	S	B
O	E	M	P	E	R	O	R	N	E	R	O	I	O
G	E	D	L	G	E	R	M	S	N	O	O	M	G
G	L	E	S	E	I	L	F	Y	O	S	I	A	G
L	N	V	E	W	B	A	C	T	E	R	I	A	L
E	I	E	M	I	N	D	B	L	O	W	E	R	I
R	W	L	V	V	U	L	T	U	R	E	S	M	N
P	C	O	E	O	G	Y	R	O	M	E	M	E	G
G	U	P	U	E	M	O	U	T	H	W	A	S	H

CAN YOU LICK YOUR ELBOW?

DEVELOP
EMPEROR NERO
SNOT
JELLYBEANS
MIND BOGGLING
MIND BLOWER
MOUSE BRAINS
SNEEZE
FUN
MIND BOGGLER
EARTH
VULTURES
MOON
GERMS
SUN
FLIES
BACTERIA
MOUTH WASH
MEMORY

Now memorise this picture then cover it.

How many houses had 3 windows?

How many windows and doors were there in total?

THE MYTH BUSTER

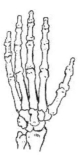
Has anyone ever told you not to crack your fingers because it will give you arthritis?
Not True.
It won't give you arthritis, but it sounds pretty painful.

Have you ever heard the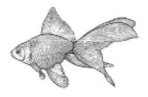

saying "goldfish only have a three second memory?"
Not true.
In fact, some researchers believe that goldfish could have a memory span of up to 5 months long.

If you pull a face and the wind blows, your face will not stay like that.

Have you ever heard people say that eating carrots will improve your eyesight? Not true.

Have you ever been told not to swallow chewing gum because it will take you seven years to digest?
Not true.
Your body will excrete it within hours or days. The ingredients in gum can't be digested so it will just pass-through during bowel movement.

Have you ever heard that your hair and nails continue to grow after death.
Not true.
The skin around them retract because they are dehydrated, which makes them look longer.

Have your heard people say that "eating cheese at night will give you nightmares". Not true.

Is it bad luck to walk under a ladder? No, it's not. But when people believe in things like this, they become more consciously aware of what is going wrong, and begin to make random connections.

The superstition originated around 5000 years ago in ancient Egypt. Apparently, ladders were left in the tombs of the dead so that they could ascend to the heavens when they were ready. The Egyptians believed that the area between the ladder and the wall was home to spirits. If the spirits were disturbed, they would be angry, so it was barred and seen as a taboo for anyone to walk under a ladder.

A black cat crossing your path, some people believe is bad luck, and others believe its good luck, but the reality is, your luck isn't affected at all. So, there is no need to spit, or to wait for someone else to cross the path first, or to alter your rout. The poor black cat has no idea why people behave so strangely around it.

Years ago, people believed that black cats were witches that had been reincarnated or, were pets that were helping witches with their evil deeds.

In Japan, it is believed to be good luck if a black cat crosses your path. In Germany, the direction in which a black cat walks in front of you determines if it is good luck or bad luck. If a black cat walks from left to right, it means good luck, but right to left means bad luck.

If a black cat appears on your doorstep in Scotland, tradition suggests you could be coming into money.

 Why are people so interested in rainbows? Is there really a pot of gold at the end of the rainbow? Wish there was, but no, there isn't. Sorry.

Have you heard the saying "humans only use 10% of their brain?"
Not true.
This is a myth. The majority of the brain is actually always active.

Have you ever heard people talk about Leprechauns, and their treasure? Have you heard them say that if you catch a leprechaun you get three wishes? Do leprechauns really live in Ireland? Well, leprechauns are fictional characters. They are make-believe but make amazing characters in stories. Sorry.

Have you heard people saying drinking coffee makes you dehydrated?

Well, can we say this is true if researchers have not found any increased risk of dehydration in coffee drinkers compared to non-drinkers.
Caffeinated drinks may cause you to wee more but they don't appear to increase dehydration.

Have you ever heard people say, If you put a chameleon on a red surface, it turns red, put it on something yellow, and it turns yellow? Chameleons Change Their Colour Depending on their surroundings? Not True.

In fact, a chameleon's mood, temperature, and the light hitting it, is what influences its colour.

Does going out with wet hair cause you to catch a cold?

No, it doesn't.

Just like being in the cold, wet hair may make you uncomfortable, and may irritate you, but it does not cause a cold. Only viruses do that.

Have you ever been told to wear a cap in the cold because our body heat escapes through our heads? Not True In fact, you just lose about 7 to 10 percent of your body heat from your head.

Have you heard people say, that a coin thrown from a great height can kill someone?

Not true.
If you were hit by the coin it would probably sting, but fatality would be unlikely.

If the coin was to hit the windscreen of a vehicle in moving traffic, then you would be in trouble. The shock of something suddenly hitting a windscreen, in moving traffic alone can cause the driver to swerve or panic.

A duck's quack does not echo.
Not true.
Actually, it does. You will need a duck and a tunnel if you don't believe me.

Shaving makes hair grow back thicker.
Not true.
When hair is shaved, it is cut straight, the end is not tapered so it makes the hair look as though it has grown back thicker.

Have you heard of the five-second rule?
Well, it's not actually true.

Even if you dropped the food on the floor for a second it would still be infested with bacteria. Sorry.

Have you heard people say that the doors and handles in a toilet are highly infested with bacteria?
Well actually, in the whole bathroom, it has the least bacteria, as it is too hard and dry for the bacteria to survive.
Have you heard the saying "lightning never strikes in the same place twice?"
-Well actually, it can strike the same place twice, as well as two places at the same time.
As a matter of fact, this is just an expression used to say that something bad happened once, but it cannot happen again.

Have you ever heard people say, "Healthy teeth should be white?"
-Wrong, a tooth's natural colour is yellowish.

If you open an umbrella indoors, your luck will not change. Although why a person would want to open an umbrella in doors, I do not know.
Opening an umbrella suddenly, in a

small room, is not a good idea. It could injure someone or break something. Even a minor accident could provoke an argument. Nothing to do with bad luck, just common sense.

And for the final question, is Santa the best toy maker in the world? The answer is, yes. He is the best toy maker ever known, along with his elves.

THE JOKESTER

THE BEST JOKES EVER TOLD.

A Buddhist goes to get a hot dog and says to the hot dog vendor "Make me one with everything,"
Then, after getting his hot dog, the Buddhist hands the vendor a £20 note.
The vendor takes the money and moves to helping the next customer.
The Buddhist looks puzzled and asks the vendor,
"Where's my change?"
The vendor replies,
"Change comes from within."

Do you know what you call a cow with no legs?
-Ground beef!

Do you know what you call a cow with two legs?
-Lean meat!

What do you call a pig that does karate?

-A pork chop!

Do you know why bees have sticky hair?
-Because they use honeycombs!

A young boy goes into a barber shop and the barber whispers to his customer,
"This is the stupidest kid in the world.
Watch, I'll prove it to you."
The barber puts a pound in one hand and 50 pence in the other, then calls the boy and asks,
"What one do you want, son?"
The boy takes the 50 pence and leaves.
"I told you?" said the barber. "That kid never learns!"
Later, when the customer leaves, he sees the same young boy coming out of the ice cream parlour.
"Hey, son! May I ask you a question?
Why did you take the 50 pence instead of the pound?"
The boy licked his cone and replied:
"Because the day I take the pound the game is over!"

Do you know what the difference is between broccoli and boogers?
-Kids don't eat broccoli!

What amazing invention gives you the power to walk through a wall?
-A door!

What did the shark say when he ate the clownfish?
-This tastes funny.

What did the bald man say when he got a comb as a present?
-Thank, I'll never part with it!

Did you hear about the hyena that swallowed an Oxo cube?
-He made a laughingstock of himself!

A climber fell off a cliff, and, as he tumbled down, he caught hold of a small branch.
"Help! Is there anybody up there?" he shouted.
A voice replied, "I will help you, my son, but first you must have faith in me."
"Yes, yes, I trust you!" cried the man.
"Let go of the branch," the voice said.

There was a long pause, and the man shouted up again, "Is there anybody else up there?"

What do you call a parade of rabbits hopping backwards?
-A receding hare-line!

Two hunters are out in the woods when one of them collapses. He's not breathing, and his eyes are glazed. The other guy whips out his mobile phone and calls 999.
"I think my friend is dead!" he yells. "What can I do?"
The operator says, "Calm down. First, let's make sure he's dead."
There's a long silence, then the operator hears a gun shot. Back on the phone, the guy says, "OK, now what?"

Every ten years, the monks in the monastery are permitted to break their vow of silence to speak two words. Ten years go by and it's one monk's first chance. He thinks for a moment before saying, "Bad Food." Ten years later, he says, "Hard bed." It's the big day, a decade later. He gives the head monk a long stare, smiles and says,

"I quit."
"I'm not surprised," the head monk says. "You've been moaning ever since you got here."

A lady tells her doctor, "Doctor, help me. I'm obsessed about Twitter!"
The doctor replies, "Sorry, I don't follow you..."
A taxi passenger tapped the driver on the shoulder to ask him a question.
The driver screamed, lost control of the car, nearly hit a bus, went up on the pavement, and stopped inches from a shop window.
For a second, everything was quiet in the taxi. Then the driver said, "Look, mate, don't ever do that again. You scared the living daylights out of me!"
The passenger apologised and said, "I didn't realise that a little tap would startle you so much."
The driver replied,
"Sorry, it's not really your fault.
Today is my first day as a taxi driver — I've been driving a funeral van for the last 30 years."

Why did the nurse need a red pen at work?
-In case she needed to draw blood!

Why aren't koalas' actual bears?
-They don't meet the koalafications!

I got my son a fridge for his birthday.
-I can't wait to see his face light up
when he opens it!

Why did the Oreo go to the dentist?
-Because he lost his filling!
Why don't you ever see Santa in
hospital?
-Because he has private elf care!

Why was the snowman rummaging in
the bag of carrots?
-He was picking his nose!

A tortoise is crossing the road when
he's mugged by two snails. When the
police arrive, they ask him what
happened. The frightened tortoise
replies,
 "I don't know. It all happened so
fast."

Why was Tigger in the bathroom?
-He was looking for Poo!

How many rotten eggs does it take to
make a stink bomb?
-A phew!

Why do gorillas have such big nostrils?
-Because they have such big fingers!

A guy notices a sign outside a house that reads "Talking Dog for Sale."
Fascinated by what he reads, he walks in.
"So what have you done with your life?" he asks the dog.
"I've led a very full life," says the dog.
"I lived in the Alps rescuing avalanche victims. Then I served my country in Iran. And now I spend my spare time reading to the residents of a retirement homes."
The guy is shocked to say the least. He asks the dog's owner,
"Why would you want to get rid of an incredible dog like that?"
The owner says,
"Because he cant stop lying! He never did any of that!"

Knock! Knock! Who's there?
Scold.
Scold who?
Scold outside, let me in.

Knock, knock!

Who's there?
Gladys.
Gladys, who?
Gladys the weekend—no homework!

Knock! Knock!
Who's there?
Needle.
Needle who?
Needle little help getting in the door!

Why did the skeleton climb up the tree?
-Because a dog was after his bones!
How did the skeleton know it was going to rain on Halloween?
-He could feel it in his bones!

Are any Halloween monsters good at maths?
-No—unless you Count Dracula!

Tim goes to his mother and asks
 "mum did you say my baby brother is an angel?"
-Yes, of course, he is
"Then why didn't he fly when I threw him from the window?"

Brother: That planet up there is Mars.
Sister: Then that other one is Pa's.

Dad-Son you're going to have a new brother.
Son – Oh my gosh does it mean mums..
Dad - No , we're giving you to another family!

My twin brother called me from jail. He started with, "So you know how we finish each other's sentences?"

Sister: Did my brother come from heaven?
Mother: Yes.
Sister: Well, I don't blame the angels for chucking him out.

How can you spell too much with two letters?
-XS (excess).

Why did your sister cut a hole in her new umbrella?
-Because she wanted to be able to tell when it stopped raining!

A boy was born in an Indian, Chinese, Irish, and Italian family. They could not settle on a name, until it hit them!
They named him Ravi O. Lee

My grandmother, who is a chef, says that I must always eat my mistakes.
-I am a surgeon!

At what time do most people go to the dentist?
-At tooth-hurty (2:30).

Can you spell a pretty girl with two letters?
-QT (cutey).

A man and a dog were going down the street. The man rode, yet walked. What was the dog's name?
-Yet!

An elephant always remembers, but what animal always forgets?
-An owl. It keeps saying, "Who? Who?"!

What cake is as hard as a rock?
-Marble cake!

What does "Maximum" mean?
-A very big mum!

How can you spell icy with two letters?
-IC (icy)!

How can you double your money?
-Look at it in a mirror!

How do you make a lemon drop?
-Hold it and then let go!

What kind of biscuit would you find at the south pole?
-A penguin!

Did you hear about the boy who slept with his head under the pillow?
-When he woke up, he noticed the fairies had taken all his teeth!
Did you hear about the parents who called their baby 'Caffeine?'
-It was a great choice of name, it kept them awake all night!

'Doctor, doctor, I can't get to sleep at night.'
'Lie on the edge of the bed, then, and you'll soon drop off.'

What do you call a dinosaur that is sleeping?
-A dino-snore!

What do you call a duck that gets all A's?
-A wise quacker!

What do you call a bull that's sleeping?
-A bulldozer!

Why didn't the monster eat the crazy person?
-He was allergic to nuts!

Why did the painting go to jail?
-It was framed!

Why did Cinderella get kicked off the football team?
-Because she ran away from the ball!

Why do we tell actors to break a leg?
-Because every play has a cast!

What does a cloud wear under his raincoat?
-Thunderwear!

Why did the kid bring a ladder to school?
-Because she wanted to go to high school!

Why was the equal sign so humble?
-Because he wasn't more than or less than anyone else!

What do you call guys who love math?
-Algebros!

Why was the math book unhappy?
-Because it had too many problems!

Why does nobody talk to circles?
-Because there's no point!

JOKES FOR THE YOUNG ONES.

What goes "Ha ha ha.....THUD!"?
-A monster laughing his head off!

What did one eye say to the other eye?
-Between us, something smells!

Have you heard the joke about the pizza?
-Never mind, it's too cheesy!

What do cats like to eat?
-Mice cream!

Why bumble bees hum?
-because they've forgotten the words!

Do you know what goes "tick, woof, tick woof"?
-A watch dog!

Can you think of something orange that sounds like a parrot?
-A Carrot!

Do you know what elves learn at school?
-The elf-abet!

How do you make toast in the jungle?
-Put it under a Grilla!

What wobbles in the sky?
-A Jelly-copter!

What do you call a blind dinosaur?
-Do-you-think-he-saurus!

How do you start a teddy bear race?
-Ready teddy go!

What do you call a fairy that doesn't like to shower?
-Stinkerbell!

Why do you think the banana went to the doctor?
-Because it wasn't peeling well!

Patient - Doctor, doctor! I don't know what to do, my daughter has swallowed my pen?
Doctor - Use a pencil till I get there.

Patient - Doctor doctor! I feel sad, people keep calling me a worm!

Doctor - Well just wriggle onto the chair.

On a Friday night, what do monsters eat?
-Fish and ships!

Patient - Doctor doctor! I feel like a bulldog.
Doctor – Since when have you felt like this?
Patient - Since I was a puppy.

Do you know where the queen keep her armies?
-Up her sleevies!

What do you call a train that's got a cold?
-Achoo-choo train!

I have a donkey with three legs, guess what I call him?
-A wonkey!

What has 8 legs, 8 eyes, and 8 hands?
-8 pirates!

Father: Why did you put a frog in your sister's bed?
Son: I couldn't find a spider.

Why is 6 scared of 7?
-Because 7 ate(8) 9!

Where do cows go on Friday night?
-To the MOOOOOvies!

Patient - Doctor, doctor! I woke up
thinking I'm a pair of curtains.
Doctor - Pull yourself together.

Patient - Doctor, doctor! I keep
thinking that I'm a bulldog.
Doctor – Have a seat.
Patient – But I'm not allowed on the
furniture.

Patient - Doctor, doctor! I think I
need glasses.
Man - You certainly do, this is a
chippy.

Patient - Doctor, doctor, I feel like a
deck of cards.
Doctor - I'll deal with you later.

My little sister is Really really really
into frozen. She's just too much.   I
told her to let it go.

Why would I put a cake in the
freezer?
- To ice it

WHO'S THE BEST?
LET'S PUT IT TO THE TEST!

Ensure each player has a pen and piece of paper each.

Get ready for the challenge.

Set yourself a time limit for each question. It can be as little as 2 minutes, or as much as 10 minutes.

You will be tested on 42 random questions to test your knowledge, lateral thinking skills, and memory.

Once you have finished, check your answers to see who the best was.

Good luck to you all!

1.	What is 7 + 92. Is it an even or odd number?
2.	Which measurement is longer? 1 metre or 34 centimetres?
3.	An electrician needs to buy 61 light bulbs. The light bulbs come in packs of 2. How many packs should the electrician buy?
4.	63 divided by ?=7
5.	2,240 pounds is equal to how many tons?
6.	A woman enters a big box department store and fills her trolley to the top. She leaves the store without paying yet no one tries to stop her. How did she get away with this?
7.	"You can swallow me, but I can also swallow you. What am I?

8.	If you take off my skin I won't cry, but you most certainly will. What am I?"
9	What has no head but does have arms and legs?
10.	Which of the following statements is true?- Pirates did really exist and still do today. Eating carrots will improve your vision. An octopus has 1 heart
11.	What fruit can you say is the most unhappy out of them all?
12.	Im black when first brought , red when you use me, and grey when my life has ended? What am I?

13.	Which of the following statements is true?- Corpse medicine contained bits of human flesh and bone. Our stomachs are actually the same size as our feet. Socks were first worn because people would buy shoes 2 sizes too big so they could get wear out of them.
14.	When Sarah was 6 years old, her sister Cindy was half her age. If Sarah is 40 years old today, how old is Cindy?
15.	How many 9's are there between the numbers one and one hundred?
16.	What do the following have in common? 28, 32, 66, 88, 12, 6, 4, 8, 100, 120, 200, 600, 1000, 2, 22, 44.

17.	What do the following have in common? 11, 65, 77, 7, 5, 9, 35, 47, 89, 97, 3, 23, 25, 111, 333,777.
18.	What do the following have in common? Red, Yellow, Blue.
19.	What do the following have in common? 2, 3, 5, 7, 11, 13, 17, 19, 23, 29, 31, 37,
20.	What do the following have in common? Unicorns, Giants, Leprechauns, The Loch Ness monster, mermaids, werewolf, trolls.

21.	What do the following have in common.- Ostrich, Emus , penguin, Greater Rhea, cassowaries.
26.	What do the following have in common? Merida, Moana, Tiana, Jasmine, Ariel, Aurora, Belle.
27.	What do the following have in common? Claude Frollo , Gaston, Ursula, Jaffar, Scar,Chernabog, Cruella De vil.
28.	What is the correct spelling? a. Leprecorn b. leprechaun c. Leperchaun
29.	What is the correct spelling? a. Mississippi b. Misisippi c. Mississipi

30	What is the correct spelling? a. Celary b. Celery c. Cellary
31.	What is the correct spelling? a. Checosavakia b. Czechoslovakia c. Czechosavakia
32	What is the correct spelling? a. Hippopotamus b. Hipoppotamus c. Hippopotimus
33.	What is the correct spelling? a. Waggamamma b. Wagamama c. Waggamama
34.	What is the correct spelling? a. Sincerly b. Sincerely c. Cinserey

35.	What do the following have in common?
	Harry, Edward, Kate, Charles, Louis, Phillip, Charlotte, Andrew, George, Elizabeth, William.
36.	There are 3 switches outside of a room, all in the 'off' position.
	One of them controls a lightbulb inside the room, the other two control other lights within the corridors. You cannot see into the room, and once you open the door to the room, you cannot touch any of the switches again.
	Before going into the room, in what order would you flip the switches in order to be able to tell which switch controls the light bulb?
37.	What is non-toxic but can kill you?

38.	Tuesday, Reyana and Jess went to the cafe. They split the £6 bill equally. What did they each pay
39.	When Nick was 8, his brother was half his age. Now, Nick is 14, How old is his brother?
40.	Can you think of 3 numbers, which give the same result when multiplied and added together?
41.	People either love me or hate me. I can change a person's appearance and thoughts. If a person takes care of himself or herself, I will go up even higher. To some people I am a mystery. You might want to try and hide me, but I will show. No matter how hard people try, I will Never go down. What am I?
42.	If eleven add two equals one, what does nine add five equal?

ANSWERS

ARE YOU READY TO SEE WHO WAS THE BEST?

ANSWERS

1.	Odd
2	Metre
3	31 packets
4	9
5	One Ton
6	The woman is an employee of the big-box company. She fills her trolley with rubbish and leaves the store to take it to the dumpster.
7	Water
8	An Onion
9	A Chair
10	Pirates really do exist. They did then and do now.
11	A Blueberry
12	I am Charcoal

13	A
14	37 years old
15	9
16	Even numbers
17	Odd numbers
18	Prime colours
19	Prime numbers.
20	Are not real.
21	All flightless birds.
22.	All red foods
23	All green foods
24	They glow in the dark.
25	Heroine
26	All Disney princesses
27	All Villains in Disney films. 101 Dalmatians -Cruella De Vil .

	Fantasia-Chernabog. The Lion King -Scar. Aladdin -Jafar. The Little Mermaid -Ursula. Beauty and the Beast -Gaston. Hunch back of Notradam- Claude Frollo.
28	B
29	A
30	A
31	B
32	B
33	A
34	B
35	Members of the royal family
36	Flip the 1st switch and keep it flipped for three minutes. Then unflip it and flip the 2nd switch. Go into the room. If the lightbulb is off but warm, the 1st switch controls it. If the light is on, the 2nd switch controls it. If the light is off

	and cool, the 3rd switch controls it.
37	Time
38	£2 (Tuesday is the name of their friend)
39	His brother is 10. Half of 8 is 4, so Nick's brother is 4 years younger. This means when Nick is 14, his brother is still 4 years younger, so he's 10.
40	1, 2, and 3 (1 + 2 + 3 = 6 and 1 x 2 x 3 = 6).
41	Age
42	11 o'clock plus 2 hours is 1 o'clock 9 o'clock plus 5 hours is 2 o'clock.

Well done to all of you.
I hope you didn't get too many wrong.

Congratulations to the winner!
The winner now gets to give each player a dare!!

Why this book is an absolute must have.

This book looks at fun and interesting ways to help your child develop in different areas, as well as interact.

Tongue twisters are established to clarify the pronunciation of words and stretch and strengthen the muscles that we tend to use to talk. They assist us to spot words and sounds we have trouble pronouncing. The more we practice, the better we get, so why not make it as fun as possible.

Brainteasers and riddles reinforce the affiliation between your brain cells, which results in a sharper short-term memory. When you play brain games, you continuously have to remember shapes and patterns, which help to strengthen your memory.

Lateral thinking puzzles have many advantages. They help us to expand our imaginative thinking skills, assisting us to develop our brain in as many ways as possible. The left side of our brain controls systematic and logical thinking, and the right-side controls imagination and creativity. When you are working on puzzles, you are using both sides and giving your brain a real mental workout.

Learning facts keeps our minds active and helps us to gain confidence to express our ideas and opinions.

Memorising facts and lists can build the foundations for higher thinking and problem solving, and most of all, can trigger interest, to make you want to learn even more.

Have you ever heard people say, "Laughter is the best source of medicine"? Jokes are an amazing way for children to connect with others. A good laugh has great short-term effects. It will energise several organs, enhances your intake of oxygen-rich air, stimulates your heart, lungs and muscles, and will increase the endorphins that are released by your brain. Laughter increases your immunity, and best of all makes you feel great.

Children who read, get better at it. Reading has so many benefits. It exercises our brains, boosts concentration, teaches children about the world around them, and enhances vocabulary and language skills. Children learn new words as they read and flip through the pages. Subconsciously, they absorb data on the way to structure sentences and the way to use words and language.

Reading helps us to expand our imagination and empathy, but the best thing about reading is, it can be amazingly interesting and fun. Once you learn to love reading, your potential is endless. Happy reading.

Most of all, this book is a must have because let's face it, apart from a games console, what can beat gross, gruesome and weird facts.

I HOPE YOU ENJOYED
THIS BOOK OF
MIND BOGGLERS.

Why not check out the next book to this series-

"CAN YOU OUTRUN
A HIPPO?"

T.K.Virdee

Can You
Outrun A
Hippo??

Did you know one of
the most deadliest
places in the world is a
place nick named
"Snake Island".

What are elephants
scared of?

What has to be
broken before
you can use it?

Did you know that
elephants can't
Jump?

What is put on a
table, but is
never eaten?

What can you
hold in your left
hand but not in
your right?

What has 8 eyes, 8
legs, and 8 hands?

Can you dig a
tunnel through the
earth to get to the
other side?

T.K.Virdee

Printed in Great Britain
by Amazon